ALL THE

DARK PLACES

A POETRY COLLECTION

Frankie Riley

I see the pain behind your eyes.
I feel the aching in your soul.
But I hope you find solace in these words,
through all the dark places.

If you are reading this right now,
in the darkness of your room,
holding yourself together,
trying to ignore the loudness
of your anxious thoughts,
to make yourself exhausted so that
sleep might just come that little bit
easier tonight.

I want you to believe that it won't
always feel like this.
Soon it will feel a little better,
then a little better, then a little better.
Day by day, the light will begin
to break through again.
You *will* survive this,
all the strength you need is within you.
Please, just keep going.

I wish I didn't know what it's like,
to lay beside someone,
yet feel more alone than ever.
But I do, I know all too well.
That complete emptiness inside.
Panic rising and clutching my throat,
every. single. night.
Suffocating me from the inside.
I never lost more sleep,
than when I was with you.
Questioning. Praying. Begging.
This couldn't be my life forever,
could it?
Like a caged bird, I longed to be free.
Your walls always closing in on me.
That's how it feels, loving an emotional abuser.
Stuck in a place,
with someone you've grown to hate.

Maybe the reason I feel
so exhausted right now,
is not because I'm in
desperate need of sleep,
but because my mind
and soul are craving peace.
Peace from the one who makes
my world feel nothing but chaotic.
The one who constantly drains me,
stealing every last shred
of my energy.

There is nothing as inherently loud as anxiety,
not more so than in the still and silent moments.
I desperately wish that my mind would just be quiet,
a brief reprieve, even for a second.
I wish I could allow myself to rest,
but there's this urgency to be busy,
to find distractions,
attempting to fill the silence in any inconsequential
way I can.
As once the silence comes,
it's just too much... *silence.*
Especially at night, when there is nothing but the darkness.
I yearn for peace,
but my mind has other ideas.
Concerns and doubts are thrust into the spotlight,
perceived failures,
and dreadful made-up scenarios that *could* happen.
The stillness turns up the volume,
anxiety at maximum capacity,
so loud that it's almost deafening,
screaming at me from within.

If you can love the wrong person so deeply,
the one who caused you profound pain and misery,
then imagine how much love you're capable of feeling
for the *right* person.
The one who will treat you in the way that you deserve.
The one who will actually be gentle with your heart.
The one who will return all the love you gave
to those who were unworthy.

It's been a while, since I saw you.
My eyes fixate on you, and I wonder…
is the person I fell in love with still there,
somewhere deep,
under all that aggression and hatred?
Your face still has some of those soft edges,
that I used to so lovingly trace with my fingers.
But your eyes? The golden warmth is gone,
replaced with darkness.
You hug me, and you still smell the same,
I take a deep breathe,
the familiar scent filling my senses.
But my body? It no longer feels safe in your arms.
The tension runs deep into my bones,
a warning sign,
my body's way of reminding me of the
pain I will endure if I give myself to you again.

I wish my mind and I could live in harmony.
But depression haunts me daily.
Overthinking, my old enemy, steals my joy.
Anxiety insists on being the loudest
voice in the home that is my body,
will it ever listen to my cries for peace?

When you look in the mirror,
I hope you say to the person staring back at you
that you are eminently *proud.*
Proud of all you had to do to survive.
Every obstacle you defeated,
just to make it to this point in your life.
The endless tears you have dried.
All the internal battles you've endured.
How much you've fought to heal from the pain,
pain you never deserved to suffer.
For bravely showing up, every single day,
even though the world is messy
and your soul aches.

You hate the word *no*.
When it comes out of woman's mouth, anyway.
I could say the F word to you
and you'd probably laugh, but *no?*
Oh, how dare I.
No is a slap in your face.
No is a lack of respect.
No is a step to you losing your control.
No challenges your idea of masculinity,
and the desirability you thrive off.

How many more times will I have to shout it
from the rooftops, before you finally listen?
"No means no."
It doesn't mean push harder,
or intimidate,
or manipulate,
or force,
relentlessly, until you get your own way.

You should not have to
sacrifice your values,
boundaries or inner peace
for your relationship to work.

Now read that again,
until it deeply sinks in.

Growth feels uncomfortable
because it's unfamiliar.
You don't know the next place,
or the new version of you.
It's equal parts scary and messy.
You must be willing to let go
of your old self, and this
life that no longer serves you.
But please don't let the fear
keep you here.

I spent so many hours wondering and doubting if I would ever be brave enough to walk away from you. I mean, for the *final* time. I loathed myself for repeatedly forgiving you, even when the rational part of my brain screamed at me for so long that I deserved better. But evidently my heart felt that it could endure your endless torture.

In the years before our lives collided, I poured all my energy into unearthing my soul from the ashes of the last person who burned me. Piecing my broken heart back together. Swearing that I would never again give someone the power to burn me in the same way.

So *how* could I let this happen? *How* could I tolerate such hurtful and disrespectful behaviour?

On the other hand, how could I have possibly understood how toxic you were, when your 'love' was so confusing. Constantly blinding all my senses, and all rational thoughts. Your words were everything you *knew* that I needed to hear. That I was loved beyond measure, safe from everything that haunted me, and promises of the family life I deeply desired. But your conflicting actions revealed that you would stop at nothing to tear our relationship apart at the seams, my heart and soul along with it.

I know it feels like your heart
has been shattered,
but the wrong person
walking out of your life
is the *best* thing
they could ever do for you.
You didn't lose them,
you were set free from a love
that was less than you deserve.

We desperately want to heal from past traumas,
but we bury our emotions rather than process them.
We crave a positive mindset,
but we constantly worry about what may
or may not happen.
We dream of the things we want to achieve in life,
but being afraid of failure stops us from chasing them.
We desire connections with others,
but instead, we keep emotionally distant out of fear.

- the battle with defence mechanisms

Millions of atoms had to come together,
forming in such a unique way,
to create every beautiful being on this planet.
So how could you ever believe that you
don't belong here?
With every breath you take,
know that you belong in this world.
You have a purpose.
You will find a place on this Earth
that feels like home,
a place where there are people
whose lives are made so much better,
simply because you exist to them.

Loving a narcissist feels like having
your brain cracked open,
everything good you've ever felt
about yourself ripped out,
and buried in the depths of the earth.
And then *you* apologise to *them*
for your declining mental state.

I understand now,
what is harder than being alone.
It's being in love with someone
who makes you feel completely alone.
They won't offer the support you need,
be a shoulder to cry on in your darkest hours,
be present through the good times and the bad.
They can't, because they don't *see you*.
Your feelings.
Your fears.
Your deepest desires.
What makes you cry.
What makes your soul beam with light.
I understand now,
the difference between being *alone*
and feeling desperately *lonely*.

It's okay if you need to pause,
to take a break from everyday life
so you can care for your mental health.
It's okay if you need some breathing space,
to make sense of your feelings.
It's okay to admit to yourself
that you're struggling right now.
It's okay to ask the people you love
for help and support.
Please let go of the guilt and shame,
so you can do what you need to do
to find your way back to yourself.
It doesn't mean that you are weak,
and it doesn't make you a failure.
It simply means that you are *human*.

Sometimes you must descend into darkness,
to truly understand the meaning of being *happy*.
To realise how sacred it is.
That all the things you thought you needed to be happy
were actually meaningless.
You finally see that pure and true happiness is
all around you,
you just have to *look*.
In the people you meet.
The places you see.
The memories you hold.
To love and feel loved in return.
Happiness is not a checklist of objects or achievements,
it's how you choose to see the world around you.

I found rock bottom once.
Or rather, it found me.
On a dark and gloomy October day,
my world so rapidly shattered around me.
The emotional pain so profound,
it blended into the physical.
Hypothetical shards of glass flying in every direction,
from the explosion of my reality.
Piercing my skin with their razor-sharp edges.
Thrown away like trash by the person who'd claimed
to love me, so coldly and callously.
Betrayed just for the pleasure of another.
Lives forever wrecked, but only one heart broke.
Mine.
Sinking to the floor, desperately gasping
for air as the sobs wracked through my body.
Wishing the ground would fall away, swallow me whole.
The pits of hell couldn't be any worse than
the torment I already felt.
Burn me alive, kill this suffering with me.
The heartache too much to bear.

I wish I knew then, what I know now.
The painfully beautiful truth behind hitting rock bottom.
That it was the prelude to my healing journey,
a necessary evil, if you will.
Sparking my most immense personal growth,
the catalyst I needed to build a life that was *my own*.
To rise from the ashes,
never again allowing someone insignificant
to burn my soul.

Maybe there is good in them,
but are they a good person for *you?*
Does being around them fill you
with peace or chaos?
A healthy relationship should give
as much energy as it takes.

I know you try to bury your emotions
because you're so afraid of being defined by them.
As if they are a flaw in your character, somehow.
Oh, how I wish you knew,
that they are not a part of you.
You merely *experience* them.
Like everything else in nature,
human emotions are beautifully dynamic.
Forever changing,
reflecting only how you feel in the present moment.
Understand that you are not a 'sad person',
you're just feeling incredibly sad right now.
You are not an 'anxious person',
you just feel anxious in this stage of your life.
You are not an 'emotional person',
you simply feel your emotions more deeply than some.

Just stop for a second.
Take a moment.
Inhale a deep breath.
Feel the air filling your lungs.
The sun caressing your skin.
The gentle breeze sweeping
through your hair.
The sweet sounds of the
world around you.
You are here.
You are living and breathing.
You have so many reasons to
keep going.

I know you're waiting for the 'right' moment to walk away,
but please don't lose yourself before you finally accept
what your heart has been telling you all along.
Leaving the person you love, the one you thought
loved you back with the same conviction,
the one you envisioned spending the rest of your
days with…Well, it will always be painful.
Regardless of the timing,
regardless of how much pain they caused you,
regardless of how deeply you *know* it's the right decision.
But you have to leave before your heart and soul
are broken beyond repair.

- stand up, walk away, close that door, don't look back.

Heartbreak is deep, at first.
It seeps into every part of your soul.
You swear that your heart *physically* aches,
your lungs constricting with each breathe,
as if you're drowning in the pain.
It's dark, and it's all-consuming.
But this is the first day,
it's fresh and raw, cutting so deeply.
Tomorrow it will hurt a fraction less.
Then a little less.
Then a little less.
Then a little less.
Slowly, but steadily.
Until one day, you are left with nothing
more than tiny flecks of pain.
A splinter from what was once
a stake in your heart.

The world has shown me, more times than I can count,
how truly dark and ugly it can be.
Even so, I *choose* to see the beauty on this earth,
the goodness in people,
the joy in the things we often overlook,
the calm in the chaos.
Perception is a choice, so I hold onto my optimism tightly.
If I choose to see a wondrous world,
then the world I see will be wondrous.

I keep drowning in
my own thoughts.
Some days I make
it to the surface,
I can finally breathe,
then a riptide of
overthinking pulls
me back under.
Some days I'm
treading water,
then a tsunami of
anxiety hits me.

It only took a few words,
words that spewed from your mouth with hate,
to shatter the illusion of *us*.
To break the trust I fought so long to build,
to kill the future you promised was ours,
to become everything you said you would never be.
And now I sit on the floor alone,
wondering if I ever really knew you at all?

It only took a few words,
words that were ice to the flame I held for you,
to pierce through my soul,
to make me question why I ever chose to love you.
And now you sit here,
playing the role of Mr. Regretful,
telling me you take it all back.
But can't you see?
Your words are carved on my heart,
like the cruelest love letter,
I remember them every time I look at you.

It only took a few words,
to kill *us*.

Despite everything you have done to me,
I still have the power of choice.
That's something you can never take
from me, my freedom to choose.
And I'm choosing to leave you.

I think one of the most profound parts of my healing journey, was understanding and *accepting* what is in the realm of my control.

The truth is, you can't control how others decide to treat you, no matter how much you try.

But you can control how you react to them, if you decide to respond with anger or kindness.

You can choose to invest in a relationship, but as hard it is to accept, you can't control whether they will invest the same effort in you.

You can choose how and when to enforce your boundaries, but you can't control whether people will respect them; although, you have the power to walk away if they don't.

You can't control when or *if* someone falls in love with you, but you can choose to fall in love with yourself.

You can't control what happened in your past, but you can learn from your experiences and decide the choices you make going forward.

You can't control the expectations that people have of you, but you can control what you expect of yourself, and ultimately how *you* choose to live.

It's okay if you
feel like your
anxiety overwhelmed
you today.
Please don't
punish yourself,
it will only get under
your skin even more.
Tomorrow will
be brighter.
Just keep going,
I promise you are
doing better
than you think.

I used to fear failure.
Fear what others thought of me.
Fear not being enough.
Until I realised my biggest fear
was letting the fear control me.
To never do anything I wanted
in my limited time on earth,
because I was too afraid.

Alcohol was always your quick fix,
you thought you could drown your feelings.
But the whiskey was like petrol,
adding fuel to the inferno inside you.
That's when your focus turned to me,
the fire exploding in my face.
You thought that maybe I was the problem,
that making me your emotional punching bag
would cool the heat of your searing anger.
That all that hate and frustration
that simmered in your blackened soul,
would somehow melt away.
Oh, how I wish you would've realised,
external things can't solve internal problems.

And still, I ask myself,
how could you be good in some ways
yet so bad in others?
As though two versions of you existed.
But perhaps there was only one,
I was just too hung up on the lie to
realise who you *really* were.

I know it sometimes hurts, to be a deep feeler.
To be consciously aware of every emotion,
feeling their presence deep within your soul.
Always wearing your heart on your sleeve,
afraid that it's too fragile to be so exposed to
this cruel world.
Hurt clinging to your bones after every upheaval,
wishing you could shake off the pain quicker.
It's so overwhelming, I know.

But what if I told you that it's not a curse,
to be a deep feeler?
That the world needs more of what you are,
because of your capacity to process everything
around you
with such wondrous depth.
You love deeper than most.
You effortlessly see into the expanse of someone's soul,
becoming highly attuned to their emotions.
Your empathy is boundless,
always showing a compassionate
understanding towards others.
You see the beauty in this imperfect world.
You are *alive with feeling,*
and that could never be a curse.

Your pain is valid.
Your feelings are valid.
Even if someone else's experience
may seem harder than yours,
it does not make your suffering
any less significant.
Please don't let anyone make you feel
guilty for feeling, just because their
trauma looks different to yours.

You did not raise me; you *chose* to walk away.
And so, I became the child who craved affection,
but was too scared to accept it.
And so, I became the teenager who was desperate for love,
but constantly searched for it in all the wrong places.
The teenager who did not dare step out of line,
for fear of rejection.
And so, I became the young woman who held onto toxic
relationships because she did not believe in her worth.
And so, I became the strong woman who healed from the
trauma you created all those years ago.

- a note to my biological father

I am ready to heal.
I have to be.
I refuse to let this trauma
keep passing down
through more generations.
I refuse to let my child
carry this burden.
The pain ends with me.

What more of me could you take,
to finally be satisfied?
Four years.
Four long years, you just sucked
out all the good from me.
Every waking thought in my mind.
Every supportive word from my mouth.
Every piece of positive energy from my soul.
Every inch of my body that you made yours.
Every fragment of my heart.
You consumed every part of me.
But still, your cup was never full.
Nothing will ever be enough for you.

I didn't mean to behave like that
I didn't mean to hurt you
I didn't realise what I was doing to you

Okay, let's look at the science, shall we?
The average human brain has at least 50,000 thoughts a day.
That's approximately 73 million thoughts over the
span of our four-year relationship.
So, you're telling me, that in any one of those thoughts,
you didn't consider my feelings?
That it never crossed your mind how much
suffering you were causing me?
That every single thought wasn't an opportunity to think
I shouldn't treat her like this?

If you could speak to your younger self, as the person you are today, what would you say?
I think the 19-year-old me, the very lost version of myself, would need my words the most.

I wish I could look into her pained eyes and tell her that she will soon realise she has so much more strength than she knows. That she *will* feel happy again, even if she doesn't truly understand what real happiness is yet.

I would want her to know that the past does in no way define her. She has the power to choose her own story, no matter how unsteady her start in life was.

I know confidence seems like an unrealistic desire to her right now, but a decade later it's as easy as breathing, once she understands that her value does not depend on the opinions of others.

I wish I could dry her tears and tell her that she doesn't have to hold onto toxic relationships out of fear of abandonment, she is worthy of real and healthy love, but first she must learn to love herself.

I would ask her to desperately hold onto that beaming optimism because there *is* good in the world, her life won't always be this dark.

If nothing else, I would tell her that I am incredibly proud of her, she fought hard to bring me to where I am today. I just need her to be patient, everything will soon make sense and she will find her path.

It's okay if you have changed.
It's okay if you have outgrown familiar places.
It's okay to no longer feel connected to the people
you thought would be in your life forever,
to realise you've grown apart rather than together.
It's okay if everything around you feels different now.
Just like the moon, you are both constant but ever-changing.
Each phase as necessary - and beautiful - as the next.

How do I know,
that they truly love me?
If they actually mean those three little words?
That they're not simply playing
some cruel game with my heart?
…like last time.

You won't need to ask, that's how.
Those desperately conflicted feelings
of yours will slowly fade,
by reason of their actions and behaviours aligning.
No confusion and questioning.
They will *show* you that they deeply love you,
without them even having to say those three little words.

One of your favourite things to tell me,
was that I needed to work on my respect for you.
That one sentence should have consumed me
with hurt and frustration...
after all, that was always your goal, wasn't it?
My pain was your fuel.
But the only reaction I could muster,
was humour.
I couldn't help but let a dark laugh escape my lips.
Because it's funny isn't it,
how the abuser could boldly accuse
the abused of having a lack of respect.
But this time, I actually did what you demanded.
I finally learned respect...
for myself,
by cutting off your access to me.

On my darkest days, I sit and wonder why
the world feels so heavy on my shoulders.
I sift through my mind, searching for some
cause or trigger for feeling so low.
But always coming up empty.
It's odd isn't it, how I can so easily overlook
all the trauma I've experienced.
As if it has no significance.
As if I don't deserve to feel hurt by it.
That's the sad truth, the more suffering we endure
the more we become desensitised to it.
Brushing it off without a second thought,
believing it doesn't deserve an emotional reaction
because it's become a normal part of our existence.

You need to let yourself feel any and every emotion, no matter how difficult they may be in the moment. Experiencing sadness, worry, guilt or fear does not mean you are falling apart, it means you are being truly honest with yourself. It's a normal part of the human existence, we are not supposed to be happy every second of the day. I know you might think you are protecting yourself but suffocating those hard emotions will only prevent your healing. All you are doing is burying them under the surface where they wait to be set free. If you never release and process your emotions you deny yourself the ability to learn from your experiences, move on and find peace. Please, give yourself permission to *feel*.

It's deeply exhausting,
being your emotional punching bag.
Your tongue is only a small muscle,
but still strong enough to break my heart.
I wish you would see,
the conflict is within you,
not with me.

You fuck up.
I cry.
I leave.
You apologise *(insincerely)*.
You make a false promise.
I come back.
You fuck up again.
Round and round we go.
I need to get off this ride,
I'm dizzy and sick.
But I can never stop
the rollercoaster,
I think I'm too addicted
to the highs.

I hope as you heal, you start to let go of
the fear of being alone,
to see it as the gift it truly is,
to learn that *alone* does in no way equate to *loneliness.*

In those still and silent moments you fear the most,
I hope you sit with your thoughts, even just for a while.
To hear the sound of your own voice.
To reconnect with your soul.
To find peace in your own presence.
To learn who you are when others are not around,
every beautiful little thing that makes you, *you.*
To embrace the escape from the expectations of others,
understanding that you are finally free to define yourself,
and how you want to live.

I hope you stay with yourself, even just for a while,
until you realise that being alone is the bravest task of all,
something to be deeply proud of,
not being alone just because you *have* to be.

On my most anxious days,
the only soothing comfort is nature.
The ebb and flow of the ocean waves,
the steady rainfall hitting the ground,
the rustling of forest trees in the wind.
It's the rhythm that helps,
the even and predictable pattern of the sounds.
They blend into my unconscious,
blocking out every other noise,
including that internal anxious dialogue
that never seems to rest.

I hope one day you believe
that you deserve the same love,
patience and empathy
that you so freely give to others.

Suddenly, I'm plunging into the deepest
depths of the roughest ocean.
This is not what I wanted; can I get out?
The tide grips me, pulling me further away.
Huge waves force my head underwater,
into the darkness, I can't see.
Cold salty water starts to fill my lungs,
I'm drowning in the pain.
I fight my way to the surface, my lungs burn
as I cough and splutter, gasping for air.
Will I ever make it out of this alive?
I try with all my might to tread water,
but I don't know if I have enough strength,
I wish this was a nightmare I could wake up from.
Then suddenly, when all hope felt lost,
the waves begin to calm,
and the tide finally loses its grip on me.
Daylight breaks through the black,
the storm passing as quickly as it came.
I'm floating now, welcoming the clean air,
the pain washing away with each breath.
I resurface, more alive than ever.

- healing after heartbreak

They say it's easy, to love.
But to love, is to be fearless.
And to keep your heart open to love,
after it has witnessed so much pain?
Well, that's a rare kind of bravery.

A song came on the radio today.
The one I used to listen to everyday on
my drive to university.
Dream by Imagine Dragons.
Oh, how I deeply connected to that song,
the line *"everything's a mess"* stuck with me,
perfectly encompassing my life at that time.
I'm so grateful for songs like this,
for their ability to transport me back in time
and realise I'm no longer that broken girl.

Your emotions serve a purpose, please listen to them.
Sadness is an expression of your depth of feeling.
Fear warns you of danger, a reminder to protect yourself.
Bitterness or resentment show that there is still healing
to be done.
Guilt signals your need to stop people pleasing.
Disappointment means that you cared enough to not give up.
Anger is an expression of your boundaries.
Shame is a sign that you should reconnect with yourself,
away from the expectations of other people.
Anxiety can signal that you're living in fear of the future.
Discomfort appears when you have the opportunity
to change, to grow, to move forward from where
you've been stuck.

Toxic relationships are like addictions,
a bad drug that you *know* is harmful to you,
but the temporary highs keep you returning for more,
a cycle you can't seem to break free from.
But the longer you stay, the more destructive they become.
Please understand that you can't medicate the pain
with the very thing that keeps hurting you.

I know you desperately want yourself back,
the person you used to be,
before you met *him*.
Before his cruel love tore into your heart.
You long to be the girl who trusted without fear,
whose view of the world was bursting with light.
But that girl went up in flames,
it's time to let her go.
And like a phoenix rising from the ashes,
you have transformed into the strong woman you
were destined to become.
Your heart may be edged with scars now,
but unbreakable.
Your view of the world a little darker,
but understanding and empathic.
Your walls a little higher,
but an unwavering trust behind them
for those who are truly worthy.
A love you only ever gave to others,
now a deep love and pride of yourself,
and all you have survived.

I step out into the cool summer evening,
lay my head on the grass,
and gaze up into the dark night sky.
The stars shine so brightly, dancing against
the backdrop of the vast universe.
Only here, staring into the infinity,
do I realise how small my problems are.

On your hardest days,
I need you to take a deep breath,
and remind yourself that
you *will* be okay.
You have been here before,
with this fear and sadness and anxiety,
but it did *not* break you.
You always end up okay,
and this time is no different,
you will survive this too,
please remember just how
resilient you truly are.

It started with harmful words,
dripping from your mouth like acid.
I didn't mean it; I had a bad day.
Then towering over me, fists clenched
at your sides, aiming to intimidate.
I'm sorry, I was angry.
It escalates.
A 'playful' slap around the back of my head.
I was just joking.
Pulling my hair as I stand up to walk away.
I don't remember that, I was drunk.
Grabbing my arms, with enough
force to leave bruises.
You know I would never hurt you.
Snatching my phone from my hands
so I couldn't call for help.
The alcohol made me lose control.
An arm around my neck.
I won't do it again.
Bruises on my body from trying to push
my way out the door, a desperate escape.
I'm sorry, I didn't mean to.
Screaming in my face, eyes wide
and full of rage.
But you know I love you.

- *the cycle of abuse*

If you truly did love me,
then why did it take me walking
away for you to finally realise
your feelings for me?
I guess you were just too busy trying
to break me to understand that
I'm worth keeping.

Please know, you don't have to
let the pain make you bitter.
You don't have to become
hard and resentful, no,
you can *choose* to soften.
Please don't let this pain darken
your sweet nature.
Remaining kind and empathic
in a painful world is the
true sign of strength.

- the kindest people are often the ones
who have experienced the most pain.

I guess it's kind of tragic,
having a biological father out there,
somewhere in the world,
whose face is unknown to me.
Never even seeing a photograph of him,
or hearing the sound of his voice.
If we passed each other on the street,
would I even recognise him?
Would he even recognise *me?*
I long to know, if we resemble at all.
My naturally mocha coloured hair
and forest green eyes, so unlike my mothers.
Did I inherit them from him?
How about our personalities, do they align?
I sometimes try to form a mental image,
but his face is blurry, never clear.
That's what eats away at me the most,
the not knowing.

The brightest things in life are often
on the other side of the darkness.
Sometimes you can't truly appreciate
the light until you first descend
into the dead of night.

I was the love of your life
until I infuriated you.
Then I became public
enemy number one.
I should've gone on the run,
instead, I let you capture me.

You were capable of love,
but you chose to be hateful.
Toxicity appealed to you more
than tenderness.
I think that truth stings me
more than anything.
You had a choice,
you chose to treat me that way.
It was a mistake, I didn't mean it
you would say.
But how could that be?
When you were capable of being
thoughtful and respectful to others.
Skilled at flashing a smile to your friends,
with the same mouth you just
used to spit venom at me.
Behaviour so cold and calculated,
always in control.
Yes, you knew exactly what you were doing,
you just didn't care.

The more I heal, the more I value peace.
A huge part of that, is being mindful and
selective of who I allow into my life.
I used to give my time, energy and heart
so freely, as though they are an endless
resource that can withstand so much misuse.
I'm now learning to surround myself with
people who are good for my soul,
while distancing myself from those who
only suck the life and energy from me.

"There is no point even trying, you will 100% fail."
"You are not good enough, and you never will be."
"Your friends and family think you're annoying,
they must be so tired of you."
"You made a mistake? Oh, your life is ruined."
"Everyone is looking and judging you, they think
you're stupid."
"WHY did you say that? Next time just be quiet."
"If you don't achieve all your goals by [insert
unrealistic deadline] then you're a complete failure."
"Don't sleep, you must stay awake all night worrying
about everything."

- lies my anxiety tells me

From as early as I can remember, I never felt like I belonged on this earth. The world around me seemed to only offer deep emotional pain and suffering. I thought I was a burden, an inconvenience, unworthy of love, just an object taking up space without any real significance. *"Why do I even exist?"* my angsty teenage self began to inwardly question, more times than I care to admit. The only logical explanation I could find at the time, was that I was not supposed to be here, living and breathing on this earth. Because I was a mistake, you see. Unwanted before I ever even took my first breath, then subsequently thrust into the foster care system. I was a glitch in God's grand plan, maybe? And this endless pain and trauma was my punishment, nature's way of reminding me just how insignificant I was, taking up space in a world that wasn't meant for me. Isn't that such an awful concept for someone to grow up believing? But as I continue to heal through adulthood, I try to remind myself daily that I am worthy of being here, living and breathing. I am learning to believe that I have a purpose, that the world needs my uniqueness. And I am slowly building a space on this earth that feels like home, with people whose lives are fuller simply because I exist to them, and vice versa. I am consciously aware that I'm just a tiny speck in this vast universe, but still, I choose to believe that *I matter.*

There's this common belief that time heals all wounds.
But I've come to understand that notion is not entirely true.
It's the steps we take *within* the time that are the true healers.
In time we don't forget the pain, rather we find ways
to live with it.
In time, we see the lessons from our painful experiences.
In time, we become stronger and more resilient.
In time, we learn how to heal our wounds.

I thought love was supposed to feel like home,
the safest place you could ever be.
Then why does it feel like I'm in a harsh
deserted land?
A war zone, sometimes.
Always searching for a way to escape.
I hope I make it out of this alive.

The stillness and silence of the forest
feels like home to me now,
the place I always run to,
my only solace from your torment.
The bird's sweet song, so contrasted to the
echo of your yelling ringing in my ears.
I have trouble breathing around you,
from those constant stabs through my heart,
piercing my lungs.
But out here, I can inhale so deeply,
like it's my very first breath on this earth.
Sometimes the rain starts to pour overhead,
I openly expose my skin to its cold touch,
I just need to feel something,
something that reminds me I'm still alive,
despite your efforts to kill me from the inside.

It's okay to feel multiple emotions,
at the exact same time.
You can feel joy, and sadness.
You can feel love, and pain.
You can feel excitement, and dread.
You can feel hope, and despair.
You can feel optimism, and anxiety.

- emotions can coexist.

Depression, for me, is to dive headfirst into the *nothingness*.
It's to look at the world around me and see only
mundane shades of grey.
There could be a lively illuminated city or a tropical
beach beaming with light,
but I wouldn't *see* it, I'm living a colourless existence.
The days are foggy, my mind always distracted,
yet no clear thoughts form.
I understand the emotions I *should* feel, but they never
reach me.
No joy or sadness, only the sensation of being numb.
The numbness seeps from my mind and into
every inch of my body,
you would think it's made of stone, unfeeling of any
human touch.
You could speak to me but mentally I'm not here,
only my physical form remains.
I meet your eyes and try to listen, but I'm not looking at you;
rather, through you.
It's as though there's a physical barrier blocking
me from the outside world
and everyone in it, yet I only want to isolate myself
even more.

If the small flutter of a butterfly's wing
can cause a typhoon halfway around the world,
then it's easy to comprehend the devastating storm
that ensued from the moment we locked eyes.

- the butterfly effect.

You knew all along, deep down.
You knew that he was not good for you.
You knew the path you were heading down
would lead to a painful ending.
But you buried that burning intuition,
and ignored the red flags,
because you had already fallen in love with him.
You'd already invested so much of your
time and energy on him.
So, you hung on.
You convinced yourself it was the right
thing to do, that maybe in time,
your intuition would prove to be wrong.
Maybe in time, he would treat you in the
way he had promised at the start.
But please know that it's never too late
to walk away, to choose differently.
To listen to that voice screaming at you
from within, even if what it's telling you is
incredibly painful to accept.
Please, trust that your soul knows what is not good for you.

I grew tired of squeezing myself into suffocating spaces that were not right for me, hopelessly searching for a place where I belonged. Always looking in the wrong areas, often in the arms of abusive men and self-serving friends. Moulding myself into something I wasn't, purely out of the deep need to be loved and accepted. But as I heal my inner child, I am learning to create my own space in this world, a space that feels like home. A space where I belong and have purpose. A space where I'm loved unconditionally. A space that erases the thought that I don't deserve to be on this earth. *A space where I can be entirely myself, for myself.*

I hope you believe that
your happiness matters too.
You shouldn't have to sacrifice
yourself and your dreams
just to satisfy someone else.

"I would give anything to go back to high school again"
I hear someone say, and instantly my stomach knots.
I feel the dread wash over me; my palms are sweaty.
I guess there are people who remember that period
of their lives with loving nostalgia,
simpler times, being young and carefree.
I'm not one of those people, and I'd give anything to
never go back to that time point again.
Those teenage years were brutal, painful,
and I was the most lost version of myself.
My introverted nature made me a target for bullies,
my kindness taken advantage of, and my optimistic
view of the world was seen as weakness.
Each day was filled with stress, fear and self-loathing.
At home there was little reprieve, living with a
drug addicted brother who was hell bent on destruction.
I was lost, depressed and painfully lonely.
I'm just so glad I didn't give up,
I'm so proud that I made it through,
and I'm so happy to say that *I'm still here.*

I have witnessed the darker side to humanity,
the immense pain and destruction some are capable of.
But I still have faith that there are billions of good,
beautiful and kind souls in this world.
I hope I never stop believing in the goodness of people.

"You're so sensitive and emotional."
"It's your fault, you always push me to act this way."
"You're overreacting again, just calm down."
"I didn't do anything, it's your trust issues messing with your head."
"You're being crazy, you need help."
"I'm sorry you feel that way."
"You don't do anything for me when I give you everything."
"You need to work on your respect for me."
"I thought my ex was a b**ch, but you're even worse."
"You always take things the wrong way."
"You should be thankful I chose you; I could have anyone I want."
"You'll regret it if you lose me, you won't find anyone better."

- things narcissists say.

Respond, don't react.
Take a deep breath,
allow the oxygen to fill you,
to reach your brain
so you can find clarity.
I know you are frustrated,
I know his words sting,
but your reaction is his fuel.
He needs your pain,
he needs your anger.
Close your eyes,
take another deep breath,
until the fog of emotion lifts.
You don't deserve the mental
toll it takes to react.
By responding, you are
in control, and you can choose
to walk away for your own
peace of mind.

Your apologies will never be enough,
they are just words, they can't undo
the pain and devastation you caused.
But I am choosing to forgive you, not so much
for you, but for my own peace and healing.
To hate takes an incredible amount of energy,
so, forgiveness helps me to find *indifference*.
You don't deserve to steal any more of my energy.

Some days, I'm tired of being strong.
Some days, I'm tired of being resilient.
Some days, I'm tired of fighting my
way through life.
Some days, I'm tired of being the
caretaker for everyone except myself.
Some days, I'm tired of carrying the
weight of the world on my shoulders.
Some days, I just wish someone would
look after my heart, mind and soul,
to care for me as much as I care for them.

You see someone friendly and talkative,
but I'm convinced you don't like me and
I'm overthinking every word I say.

You see someone who is organised,
but I feel out of control if things are not 'right'.

You someone who pays attention to detail,
but I fear making mistakes and being a failure.

You see someone who is hardworking,
but I'm my own worst critic and think I'll never
be good enough.

You see someone who is self-sufficient,
but I'm afraid to ask for help.

You see someone who is active, always on the go,
but I can't sit and relax because overthinking haunts me.

You see someone peaceful and calm,
but there is chaos raging inside my mind.

- anxiety is invisible.

I know that you so desperately want to
be accepted, to fit in.
But I hope in time you realise that
everything that is different about you,
is also what is the most beautiful.
Please understand that the world needs
more of your uniqueness.

I thought the strongest feeling
I had for you was love,
but it turns out it was actually *fear*.
Maybe fear is what I felt from the start,
maybe my brain confused the two.
After all, it has the same physiological
response as love.
The only thing I'm sure of,
is that I should've never felt afraid of
the one who claimed to love me,
the one who promised to protect me.

Please don't stay with someone who is unworthy of your love. Don't ignore how they make you feel just to keep them in your life, the temporary highs will never outweigh the persistent lows. I know it's hard to let go, but the pain of walking away will hurt less than a lifetime of unhappiness with someone who does not appreciate you. Someone who convinces you that you're difficult to love. Someone whose presence makes you feel alone, even though they are right beside you. Believe that there is more out there waiting for you, a love that won't break you down. A love that feels safe, like home. A love that inspires your soul. A love that makes you feel worthy. Please don't settle for anything less, you don't deserve to only be half loved by someone.

I spent most of childhood, and early adulthood, feeling nothing but anger towards the man who walked away before I was born. The man who refused to even acknowledge that I was his daughter, his own flesh and blood. But I am slowly learning to release the anger I held onto for so many years, for my own peace of mind.

I am slowly learning to accept that there is a part of me, deep in my soul, that will maybe never fully heal from his abandonment. But I can't allow this to hold me back, I need to continue living *through* my healing journey.

I am slowly learning that pain is a gift. The pain of his choices taught me that I can experience the anguish of rejection and trauma, and still survive. Not only survive, but also *thrive.*

I am slowly learning that my strength is incomparable, never wavering through every struggle life throws at me. No matter how much I'm pushed to the edge, I never break.

I am slowly learning that my unsteady start in life fueled me to work hard and create the life I have today, a sense of determination to give my future children everything I never had.

I am slowly learning the true meaning of family, that it is more about souls connecting and loving one another unconditionally, and not so much about sharing the same DNA.

I am slowly learning to be thankful for the pain, for it has made me into the person I am today.

It's too heavy, to keep carrying
that dark cloud hanging over you.
Please know that it's okay to cry,
you need to release the pain.
The sky never apologises for
crying on its greyest days,
so, neither should you.

I made the fatal mistake of idealising you,
putting you on an extremely high (*and unrealistic*) pedestal,
and all it did was make me blind to the red flags.
Perhaps I idealised our whole relationship,
just to rationalise the decision to keep you in my life,
despite the immense pain.

You were in self-destruct mode.
I tried so hard, but I couldn't fix you,
because you didn't want to fix yourself.
My light faded with every fight,
and if I stayed with you,
you would have continued to drag me
down into the dark pit with you.
I had to save myself.

Anxiety is a peace thief. Anxiety is a happiness thief.
Anxiety is constantly having a feeling of dread, deep
in your gut, that something terrible is about to happen.
You can't enjoy the pleasurable moments of life,
when you're always on high alert.
You can't be excited about the future,
when you're constantly battered with waves of dread,
washing away all peace and happiness.
And when you can't figure out what is wrong,
you start to think that you're the problem,
that the chaos you feel is your own fault.

I know that pushing your feelings down to the dark depths of your unconscious might make you feel better in the moment. But the truth is, you are not protecting yourself from those painful feelings, you're actually causing self-sabotage by allowing them to stick around longer than necessary. You can't truly move forward with your life, when the weight of those repressed emotions constantly pull you back to past traumas. If you never give yourself the time and space to truly *feel* and process your emotions, then you prevent the crucial understanding that facilitates healing and growth. Please understand that emotional processing is not the enemy, it's like an immune system that protects us from future distress.

Forgiving you repeatedly was like walking head
on into traffic and expecting not to get hurt.
I should have believed you, the first time you
showed me how truly dangerous you are.
Instead, I became a willing accomplice to my
own habitual heartbreak.

Why do I keep going back to him?
Because you desperately want to believe that
the one you love is inherently good,
that they embody everything you ever wanted.
So, when the reality paints a different picture,
you simply can't accept it.
Or rather, *you don't want to.*
It goes against the deep belief you have
already developed about that person.
It's incredibly hard to change that belief,
so, you skew the facts, or undermine how truly
toxic their behaviour is.

- cognitive dissonance.

I'm torn between keeping my heart open,
and locking it in a vault and throwing away the key.

There came a point in my healing journey where I started to question my decision making. Why did I choose to enter relationships with people who I *knew* were not good for me? Why did I continue down the path of destruction by *allowing* them to cause me so much heartache? Why didn't I walk away sooner? Why did I not try to heal my childhood trauma until now? Why did I make reckless decisions based on my insecurities?

As I heal, I'm learning to trust myself. I'm learning to trust my judgements. I'm learning to forgive myself for the choices I made when I was in survival mode, before I started to heal my broken parts. I'm learning that I am incredibly brave for trying, even if something failed. I'm learning that the choices I have made brought me to where I am today, and the person I am today. I'm learning that even though I've hit a few dead ends, I have accomplished some incredible things on my path so far. I'm learning to see the beauty and wonder of my journey, and to believe that I'm going in the right direction, even if I sometimes feel lost.

Pain has an evolutionary purpose.
It helps us to be aware of the things
in our environment that are
simply not good for us, to guard
ourselves against them, and to guide
our behaviour going forward.
Please understand that pain is not
the problem, it's part of the solution.
It's how we learn. It's how we adapt.
It's how we grow.
Embrace the pain.

On the surface,
I'm a confident and strong woman.
And every day, I try to convince
myself that I truly am her.
But on the inside, deep in my soul,
I'm still that scared little girl.
The girl who feared abandonment,
the girl deprived of early attachments,
the girl terrified of rejection,
the girl who was desperate for love.
I hope one day,
my outside seeps through my skin,
into my mind, into my blood, into my bones.
All the way down, until I finally believe that
I am a confident and strong woman.

The sad truth is, people measure human behaviour
by their own standards.
So, you accept toxicity, because over time your
negative experiences have
lowered your standards, so much so that
unhealthy behaviour seems normal.
*I hope as you heal you learn to love and respect
yourself again.*

The alcohol didn't force you to abuse me.
No, it did not change your character.
It just gave you the confidence to release
the monster that was hidden
under your skin all along.

Here comes my anxiety again,
to fill my head with more lies.
But perhaps they're not lies?
I'm struggling to tell the difference
anymore, between what is anxiety
and what is my intuition.

If my life was a script,
played as a movie with fictional characters,
I would undoubtedly sob ugly tears
into my cinema popcorn.
But this is no movie, this is my life.
Yet my ability to feel empathy or compassion
for myself is nonexistent,
as if my own trauma is not painful enough.
So, I delve into sad movies for an emotional outlet,
something to make me *feel*,
to release the pent up emotions I've suppressed.
Breaking the dam, allowing the tears to finally flow
- *even if they are not tears for myself.*
How is it that my empathy for others is the only
thing that can break through the numbness I feel?

It took me a while to understand how afraid you have
made me, that my reactions are not natural behaviour.
Since you, I see the enemy everywhere I look.
Peering through the door before I dare leave the house.
Jumping out of my skin at every loud noise.
My heart stopping every time I hear my doorbell.
Even walking in the serene forest, I always glance behind
me cautiously searching for potential threats.
My trembling body is forever on high alert,
I can't turn it off.
I'm haunted by you; the fear runs deep in my bones.

- PTSD after domestic abuse.

The mind may forget, but the soul does not.
Our minds are an etch-a-sketch, easily wiping away
and repressing painful moments - *to protect us.*
But we still feel the pain deep in our souls.

Having a deep-rooted fear of rejection can keep you hanging onto people - family, friends, lovers - that are incredibly toxic for you. You would *do* anything, and *be* anything, just to keep them in your life. You don't stop for a second to even consider if they are good for *you*, and how they truly make *you* feel. Your whole motivation - often subconsciously - is to please them, to gain their love and acceptance. I really hope as you heal your inner child, you start to remember that your self-worth is not dependent on the approval of others.

Please, don't keep torturing yourself
about whether you should stay or leave.
Ninety five percent of our decisions are made
in the subconscious, so you have already
made your choice, it's just a matter of
consciously accepting it.

I'm sorry, I didn't mean it.
How can I believe you, apologies are nothing
without change.
I will never behave like I did all those other times.
You are what you do, not what you say.
I promise I will never hurt you again.
Your promises are as empty as your heart.

That's the danger of nostalgia, it clouds our judgement. When we revisit past relationships, we often only remember the good parts of it, our brain seems to conveniently forget the bad. Or because some time has passed, the lows don't seem so bad or painful now. Our memory distorts, painting the experience in a way that is more positive than the reality. So, we must challenge our recollection and ask *"was that really how it felt, being with him? Was I even happy?"*

We're psychologically wired to favour routine and patterns, so when we suddenly experience a big change or upheaval, our brain deceives us into thinking this new phase of our lives is negative or too difficult. It desperately searches for that familiar routine, because it's easy, predictable and stable. But when you push through that brief discomfort, the fog of the nostalgia will subside. Allowing you to finally see the relationship for what it was, not what you *thought* it was.

I just don't understand
why my anxiety is so bad lately.

She asks whilst carrying around
an enormous Pandora's box,
overflowing with her unresolved trauma.

I know these days are hard.
Life feels messy, complicated.
As if the whole world weighs
heavily on your shoulders.
Chaos invades your mind,
making you ache for peace.
But please believe that it
won't always feel like this.
You just have to keep going.
Put one foot in front of the other,
take a deep breath,
and keep going.
Peace will find you.

In every good moment in my life,
you ripped through like a tornado,
hell bent on destroying my joy.
Family gatherings, holidays, new jobs
always ended up in tears, *my tears.*
It became a toxic pattern,
because your happiness was dependent on
being the better one in the relationship.
The centre of attention.
The most successful.
'The King' as you so boldly put it.
In your eyes, we could never be equals.
You needed the power and domination,
it was your oxygen.
My success was your frustration.
My happiness was your anger.
My pain was your fuel.

You were never mad at yourself
for hurting every part of me,
so, what gives you the right to be
mad at me for finally leaving you?

In my garden, stands a half dead tree,
that looks as glum and lifeless as me.
Brown wilting leaves,
soil dry beyond belief.
Do I try to bring it back to life,
or is the damage simply too rife?
I realise this tree,
is a reflection of me.
A lack of care has left it injured,
just like my soul that is incredibly splintered.
But if you pour water on my bones,
will I rise out of this lifeless zone?
Maybe soaking up the sunlight,
will take me out of this dark pit and into the bright.
Is there hope for me,
or will I continue to wilt just like the tree?
I desperately hope I come back to life,
after the one I loved cut my heart with a knife.

Every time my heart breaks,
the walls around it get higher.
A fortress made of steel, I wonder
if I will be trapped behind it forever.
I'm afraid that if I ever love again,
they will need a bulldozer to
break through my defences.

I am an ocean,
so much of me unknown to the world,
a mystery never explored.
Equal parts dark and beautiful,
chaotic and calm.
Only those who are fearless enough to dive deep,
will see the depths of my soul,
the hidden world inside of me.
But most only want my surface,
the peaceful waves,
the beaming reflections of sunlight.
To just dip their toes in the shallows,
leaving whenever the clouds start to roll in.

You forced me to
shrink and shrink
until I was nothing but a
shadow of my former self.

*It's time for me to step out of
the shadows and into the light.*

I'm too sensitive.
I guess I shouldn't take things so personally.
Maybe it's just all in my head.
Am I crazy?
It's not that bad, I'm just overreacting.
I'm not good enough.
It's fine, other people have it worse.
He didn't mean it.
I'm being too needy.
It's my fault, I'm asking for too much.
He was just joking; I need a better sense of humour.

- what gaslighting myself sounds like.

I still don't understand, why peace never appealed to you.
so many times, I waved my white flag,
"You win you win I give up, please stop"
But you would never surrender, never cease fire.
You wouldn't stop until you destroyed every single
part of me.

Yet *you* still don't understand why I'm so afraid of you.

I know it's hard to let go,
but you're not letting go,
not really,
because you already did.
You're just finally in a place where
you are able to consciously
accept what has already gone.

I've come to understand that a failed relationship
does not mean *failure*.

I've come to understand that learning what is *not* love,
is just as important as learning what *is*.

I've come to understand that I'm not starting over as the
person I was before, I'm starting over with *experience*.

Insomnia.
Migraines.
Trembling.
Exhaustion.
Tight chest.
Palpitations.
My body screams at me, when my
anxiety is getting out of control,
overwhelming every inch of me.
It's not only mental anymore,
I feel it's haunting presence in my body.

I'm learning to trust the forces of the earth,
to stop resisting, to allow the waves of life
to pull me in any direction.
Sometimes it's confusing and scary,
but I know it's taking me to where I need
to be, to my true purpose that has been
calling out to me all along.

I wasn't innocent in our downfall. You were destructive with your emotions, but I was often ice cold, trapped behind my defence mechanisms. Some days I could *feel* the emotional barrier around myself, as if I'd held onto it for so long that it now had a physical presence. An impenetrable emotional prison. I completely convinced my mind that if I committed everything to the relationship, then I would be giving you the power to sabotage me. But, in reality I was playing a part in sabotaging myself, my happiness and our relationship by being so reluctant to drop my defensiveness.

The truth is, if you always keep
your loved ones at arm's length,
an imagined 'safe distance',
then you deny them the opportunity
to see the *real* you.
To wholeheartedly feel their love,
and give yours in return.
To build a deep emotional connection
that will survive the ages,
not just brief and surface level.
Please understand that there is beauty,
courage and joy in vulnerability.

One of your favourite games is to
convince me that I can't live without you.
Oh honey, that's a bet you will never win.
I survived before you,
and I will survive after you.
The odds are in my favour.

The moment I realised
that I had truly moved on,
was when I replaced
hate with *indifference*.

I've come to understand that learning and practicing emotional intelligence is immensely challenging for those of us who have experienced trauma from an early age. Yet, it's a fundamental part of the healing journey. Sometimes I'm so aware of my emotions, I remain open to truly *feeling* them, and carefully try to make sense of their meaning. Then other times I realise I've just been going through the motions of life, whilst feeling nothing but numbness. I don't know how many days or weeks have passed on autopilot, but those repressed emotions have been slowly building inside of me. I only start to notice when they're ready to burst at the seams. Inevitably - and often for the smallest reason - that dam eventually breaks releasing a flood of emotions all at once, and I'm back to feeling overwhelmingly broken. I guess this is why they say healing comes in waves.

Two of the hardest - but greatest - lessons I
have ever learned:

*1. Sometimes the hard thing and the right thing
are the same.*

2. What feels like the end is often the beginning.

You mistook my softness for weakness.
In your eyes, I was too gentle and sensitive.
You thought you could beat me down
with your rough and hard persona.
Oh, how wrong you were,
I am both soft and strong wrapped into one.

I know that your kind heart tries
to see the best in everyone,
to believe that there *is* good in them.
You have so much empathy, and that's
a beautiful thing.
But please understand that you can't have
empathy without also having *boundaries*.
Without them, self-destruction ensues,
because your empathic heart will always
justify them hurting you.

The endless doubt and questioning
that comes with being anxiously attached,
is nothing short of exhausting.

Does he still love me?
Is he mad at me?
What if he leaves me?
I'm not good enough for him, am I?
Will he find someone else?

Trauma tends to stick to your bones,
it becomes a part of you.
Sometimes you can't tell where you end,
and the pain begins.
But the goal is not to 'get over it',
it's to continue your journey *in spite of it*.
To embrace this new version of yourself,
so, the pain is no longer in control.
To learn how to *live* again,
and not just survive.
To wear your scars with pride,
a reminder of your courage and strength.

The best thing you ever did
was tell me I couldn't do it.
Did you think I would listen?
Oh honey, I was born stubborn.
Your doubt was my fuel,
it made me work ten times harder.
Not so I could prove you wrong,
but so I could prove to myself that
I *can* do it.
I *can* achieve my dreams.
I *can* create the life I deserve.

I knew I had made the right
decision to cut ties,
when I realised that losing
you hurt so much less
than being with you.

      - clarity.

Healing did not suddenly happen the day you walked away,
it came slowly in the moments after.
Healing was in the messy in-betweenness of the
then and now.
In the time you spent alone, overcoming the discomfort,
and doing the hard inner work.
In the nights you cried yourself to sleep,
but still had the courage to get up the next morning,
with a hope that the following days would be better.
It was learning to open your heart again,
despite the fear of it being broken once more.

I've decided I don't want to be a victim anymore.
I don't want to keep living that same story,
reliving the pain of the one who hurt me.
Today it's just a story, it's not happening anymore.
So, I can tear out those pages, and set them alight.
Now I get to write my own narrative.
Now I get to tell the tale of how I healed.

When you first laid eyes on me,
you saw a timid little mouse.
Unconfident, fearful.
Someone you imagined you could
so easily dig your claws into.
To dominate and tear down.
Someone to be your dependent,
whose only purpose in life
was to meet your demands.
Your ideal prey.
But little did you know,
I was a lion all along.

And then I realised, love is not supposed to
be this crazy all-consuming thing.
It shouldn't constantly feel like a storm of emotions
raging inside of you, love should give you *peace*.
The control, jealousy, fights and endless chaos,
you convinced me that they were proof
of how deeply you loved me.
But now I understand that love shouldn't
Be incredibly hurtful and destructive.

We were always on opposing
sides of the colour wheel,
our pigments never meshing.
Cold steel grey
and warm honey amber,
would constantly clash.
I wanted our love to be art,
but the picture was always messy.
We were never art, we were chaos.

The little bird,
tattooed on my wrist,
the favourite part of my skin.
A forever reminder,
that I too am free.
Free from the cage you
forced me to live in.
Free to breathe,
without fear.
Free to spread my wings,
and live life on
my own terms.

You deserve the kind of love that makes you feel
worthy of love.
The kind of love that is patient, caring, and honest.
A love that doesn't make you think that you're asking
for too much,
or that you're too difficult to love wholeheartedly.
A love that listens and respects you.
The kind of love that fills your entire body when
they look at you.
A love that chooses you, every. single. day.
through the difficult times as well as the euphoric.
You deserve the kind of love that you always give to others.

Maybe you're having
to wait longer
because the future
that's coming for you
is even more profound
and beautiful than
you imagined.

Please don't give up hope.

For so long, I've been running away
from writing these words.
I've made myself busy. I've procrastinated.
Because I know the creativity will open up
old wounds, painful growth, and a whole
other level of who I am.
The busyness is simply a distraction,
a way to avoid my deepest thoughts,
to stop myself from digging too deeply.
I'm afraid of the depths of my mind and heart,
what will I find in there?
It feels like dangerous territory,
cracking open a pandora's box,
allowing all my emotions to spill out at once.
Like an erupting volcano,
they'll flow like lava, scorching my skin.
But I need to write, *it is my way of feeling.*
It is my way of understanding.
These words open old wounds,
but I need them to make sense of my emotions,
to make sense of my demons and desires,
to make sense of my life.

We cannot be selective about
which emotions we want to feel.
If you suppress one emotion,
you suppress them all.
So, without sadness, there would
be no happiness.
Everything in nature exists
with perfect duality.
The light does not exist without the dark.

That first sip of coffee on a Sunday morning,
foams of milk like clouds touching my lips.
Listening to the downpour on a rainy evening,
rhythmically beating against my window.
Stepping outside for a moment,
tilting my face to feel the rain droplets on my skin.
Reading a good book in a cosy coffee shop,
the smell of freshly baked croissants invading my nose.
My favourite song playing on the radio while driving,
singing along to every word, not caring if it's off key.
Strolling deep into the forest on a warm day,
letting mother nature blissfully fill my senses.
Hugging the one I love, their familiar scent enveloping me,
feeling the tension of the day leaving my body.
I see now, these small moments were never small at all.
These moments are joy, in its simplest form.
These moments give me light on my darkest days.

I'm a dreamer, I think deeply about everything.
Sometimes my mind floats in the clouds.
I'm an eternal optimist.
I cry at movies, both happy and sad.
I'm an empath, I feel *everything* around me.
I often feel my feelings too deeply.
I get excited by the smallest things.
I'm an introvert, I crave the quiet to recharge.
Sometimes I'm awkward and say foolish things.
I love with the entirety of my heart and soul.

And I'm finally learning to love who I am, unapologetically.

I used to think that I had to be completely whole
and healed for someone to love me again.
That I had to cover up my scars,
even though they are a part of me now.
To act as though I've never experienced trauma,
just so they didn't think I was too difficult to love.
But I'm slowly learning that this scarred version
of me is still worthy of love.
The fractured parts of my heart do not mean
that I am *damaged goods.*
I still have so much love to give,
and I deserve someone who can love every
part of me in return; *the light and the dark.*
To look at the parts of me that are edged with scars,
with pride in their eyes, not pity.
I am not fundamentally broken, like everything
else in nature I am *beautifully imperfect.*

I hope you know that you can take the darkest time
in your life and still turn it into something positive.
Just like the creation of our planet, it's possible for
something beautiful to emerge from a chaotic storm.

- my final words to those who are reading this.

FRANKIE RILEY is a British author.

frankieriley.co.uk
instagram.com/itsfrankieriley
tiktok.com/@wordsbyfrankie
medium.com/@frankie-riley

Printed in Great Britain
by Amazon

37117933R00086